Everything Know About Being a Better Wife

Jennifer N. Smith

CONTENTS

Everything You Need to Know About Being a Better Wife

Introduction

It takes two to tango, but women are typically considered the more emotionally intelligent of the sexes. That might explain why you are reading this book right now. You know that you and your husband love and care for each other, but maybe there is something that you know is lacking. A gut feeling or your intuition is screaming to you that there is a lot of things that could be changed for the best results in your marriage as possible. Or maybe you feel like you give your husband a hard time and can't figure out why.

Whatever reason you chose to pick up this book, one thing is certain – you want to be a better wife. There are many elements that need to combine to create the perfect marriage, and if you are thinking that there are things you can do to spice up your marriage and improve your relationship, then this is the book for you!

Many wives grow tired and resentful, causing straining relationships between themselves and their partners. Everybody has limits to what they can take, and if you feel you are reaching yours, tensions will always be high. This means that you and your partner are more likely to squabble and have a harder time getting along and maintaining a rewarding relationship.

Using the tips and tricks available to you in this book, you will not only learn ways to be a better wife, but you will without a doubt encourage your partner to be a better husband as well.

you're going to be well prepared for whatever comes your way!

Fortunately, there is an answer. Using this book, you will be able to learn all you may need to know about improving your relationship. Marriage only works when both of you are committed to making the changes that need to be made so that you can continue to be a harmonious couple. **if you are willing to work on yourself and really be honest with yourself about your own faults and the ways you, too, can be a source of conflict, then there is a great chance that you and your partner will be able to work through any difficulties so that you can reclaim the loving relationship that made you**

believe in your marriage in the first place.

In this book, you will learn all about how to trust yourself and your partner, seek confidence and confirmation in yourself, learning how to be honest with yourself and your partner so that you can both work together to make the most of your time together. If you're not able to communicate your needs and learn to compromise, you are bound to hurt yourself in the process of trying to make your marriage work.

Using the tips and tricks available to you in this book, you will not only learn ways to be a better wife, but you will without a doubt encourage your partner to be a better husband as well. If you are able to honestly communicate your needs, there is nothing that will get in your way!

Making a marriage is more than just saying "I do." There are years and years that come after that to think about, and with this book on your side, you're going to be well prepared for whatever comes your way!

Chapter 1 – The Importance of a Wife's <u>Honesty</u>

Something a lot of women forget is how to be honest with themselves and everyone around them. As a society, women are often ignored and neglected, told to nurture others and put themselves last. Women become fairly comfortable lying not only to ourselves, but to others as well when it comes to our own needs. We want to be able to take care of everybody else so much that it can be difficult to discover our own needs and avoid burnout.

But avoiding burnout is one of the most important things you can do if you are going to improve your marriage. When either party of a marriage feels burnt out, they are far less likely to uphold their obligations toward each other. This can even be reflected in the household. Every day can begin to feel like a chore, and the spark can quickly leave the marriage.

If you believe you are always right or always innocent and want to go down defending yourself until the end, it might become too much for your partner to take and it could cause serious damage to your marriage.

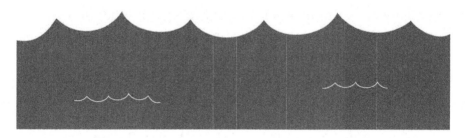

Burnout is the first step on the road to bitterness and resentment, which can seal the fate of a poor coupling faster than you would believe.

And so, it is a huge priority for women to learn how to listen to themselves once again and be honest about how they feel. This has many benefits, and you will even find that often, the men in a woman's life can be more likely to feel exasperated when women are not able to speak up for themselves. Although it seems like men like to be in control, a lot of the time they are completely fine with women taking the reins – especially when it comes to a woman's needs. If a woman knows herself and doesn't hide behind propriety or nurturing other people and neglecting herself, a man's job is that much easier. **He knows what to expect from his wife and they are both happier for it.** She is happy to be honest and not have to hide what she needs, and he is happy to avoid all the guesswork!

There is another benefit to honesty that many people don't realize. We lie to ourselves frequently. We might not like to believe it, but we each **have flaws** that can drive other people up the wall, **and if we are able to admit it instead of denying it**, then we can make progress in improving ourselves and **becoming an easier person to be around.**

No, that doesn't mean you should compromise your needs and always assume other people are right all the time and you never have grounds to be angry. However, it can be difficult for you to get along with your partner if you are never able to admit to your own faults. But admitting to your faults isn't the only step, or even the most important, though it is a great start. In order to really make honesty count, you have to really let your flaws sink in. Accept these things as weaknesses that you have so that you can both begin to move on together.

That isn't to say you should let your man blame you for every problem in your marriage so that he doesn't have to try. The exact opposite is true. You need to look at yourself and honestly examine the impact that you have on others in order for this method to work. You also have to be honest about how others affect you. It's important that this process isn't done alone, or only by looking at yourself. There are dynamics that we live in that affect our day-to-day lives, and these dynamics are extremely stressful sometimes. If we are assuming we are the only cause of any problem, that is also a problem. You are not the only one to blame, but you may be the only one to be able to be honest and objective about your situation so that you and your partner can make the changes you need toward a healthier lifestyle together. You have to be willing to make sacrifices, including being willing to see yourself in the less than glorious light that we tend to perceive ourselves in.

Next comes the fun and rewarding part – you work on these flaws. Sometimes this can even require intensive emotional work or therapy, but this is the most important part. You have to change the way you react to things in order to make any lasting differences in your life. If you discover something about yourself that you don't like and would like to change, be honest about it and embrace the flaw so that you can embrace the change!

Flaws are not inherently bad. They are more like weaknesses that we need to build up muscle for so that we can do better. We have to exercise and practice doing more strongly in our weak areas. One way to do this is by taking accountability for your flaws. You can do this by telling them to your partner and admitting your mistakes when you make them instead of going into another cycle of negativity or fighting. It can be a relief to stop defending yourself for once and really listen to what your partner has to say. **If you believe you are always right or always innocent and want to go down defending yourself until the end,** it might become too much for your partner to take and it could cause serious damage to your marriage.

Avoiding burnout is one of the most important things you can do if you are going to improve your marriage. When either party of a marriage feels burnt out, they are far less likely to uphold their obligations toward each other.

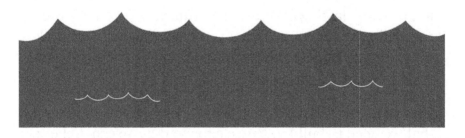

Share the things that you want to change with your husband as you discover them so that he can be patient with you as you make the transition into becoming the person that you want to be. You should initiate a conversation about how your flaw has affected him and validate him when he points out that he is being hurt by your flaws. ***Another important step in this process is to apologize.*** You tell him that you'd like to work on whatever it is that is troubling him and creating problems between the two of you. Maybe you can even ask his advice in how he might want you to deal with this particular flaw, and open up a conversation about how you can both do better for each other and accept the ways that you are lacking so you can move through them together as a couple.

Finally, when we talk about honesty we must also talk about

forgiveness. Before you approach your partner, you have to be willing to accept your flaws, yes, but also to **forgive yourself for them.** We are all human and we are raised a certain way and affected by the things in our lives that have happened to us. Each of us has a past and a story that still affects us to this very day. But to truly move on from the impact of our past, we have to forgive ourselves for them. Even if it's not our fault, we have to be willing to forgive ourselves and the people who have done us wrong so we can move forward. This is a big step that can be aided by therapy.

Sometimes we have very unforgiving partners, so admitting to our flaws can be scary and they can make us feel like we will not be forgiven for them. This is not the kind of thing that makes for a healthy relationship, but if you are going to deal with someone spiteful and petty as a husband be sure not to put yourself into a vulnerable position. What matters here is that we are able to forgive ourselves for our flaws and continue to working on them to make our lives better.

However, if you have a reasonable partner, forgiveness is a huge step toward feeling comfortable being honest when we make mistakes. Many of us are terrified of punishment or abandonment, so we will do our best to pretend that there is nothing to be angry about and try to avoid the hard conversations all together. If you can create a healing and forgiving environment where you can feel safe being honest with one another, confident in the fact that you will embrace change and forgive each other for your mistakes, there is nothing more powerful that could help you to improve your marriage!

Chapter 2 – Building <u>Confidence</u> in Yourself to Improve Your Marriage

Many women are raised to lose confidence in themselves as they grow. Children are often to be seen and not heard, and this can have a lasting impact on the psyche. If we are not able to examine ourselves and express our needs with confidence, they will never be met. And if you are going to try to work with someone, a life partner, throughout all the ups and downs of your life, you will need to know yourself and have the confidence to express the things you want and need.

Many women wouldn't recognize confidence as a way to become a better wife, but when you are confident in yourself, you are able to express yourself without any inhibitions. This is important because when you lack confidence in yourself, your needs are often not met or heard and this can create a lot of marital problems. When we feel like our partners don't hear us, then we are prone to building up resentments that can be very difficult to overcome.

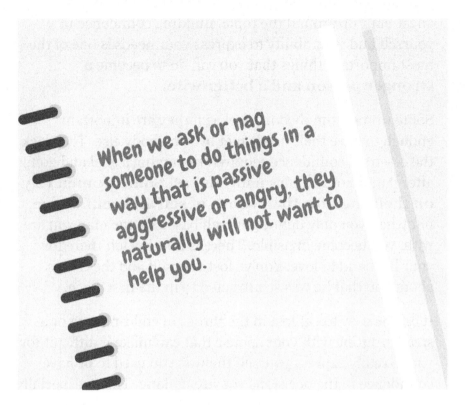

When we ask or nag someone to do things in a way that is passive aggressive or angry, they naturally will not want to help you.

These resentments can lead to petty arguments and even big ones, especially if you build up your anger and never express it until you finally get the chance to fight about something important.

These kinds of resentments can sometimes destroy a marriage and make women surly and impatient with their partners and their incompetence or inconsideration. **But have you stopped to think whether or not you are clear with what you need and why? Are you able to express yourself with confidence in a non-confrontational manner that will make your partner want to help you?** <u>When we ask or nag someone to do things in a way that is passive aggressive or angry, they naturally will not want to help you.</u> They will feel put off by your attitude, not understanding why you have so much angst built up around the topic. Building confidence in yourself and your ability to express your needs is one of the most important things that you can do to become **a stronger person and a better wife.**

Some women simply don't feel as if they are important enough to have their needs met by somebody else. They lack the essential confidence required in naming a goal and going after it and not stopping until it is met. **Some women rely on their men for their sense of self and confidence,** but when you only define yourself based on the man you are with, you become invisible. There is nothing left there for your husband to love. You've lost yourself and the things about you that he was so attracted to in the first place.

It can be easy to get lost in the throes of child-rearing or a steady routine with your spouse that can make it difficult for you to really express yourself the way you used to or have confidence in the decisions you are making. This is especially easy to understand when your decisions have consequences to other people, such as your partner or your children. We lose confidence in ourselves and also lose a grasp of what is important to us. **We get used to putting other people first and second-guessing it whenever we are put in a position to make a choice that will be good for us versus what might be good for someone else or a collective whole.** However, losing this confidence also often means losing ourselves in the process. And this is one of the biggest problems in many marriages. Women aren't confident in themselves and begin to lose the **unique spark of who they are.** They become almost caricatures of who they once were when they fell in love with their partners and because of this the marriage suffers.

This can happen for many reasons. In fact, a lot of men seem to expect this type of submission. And we can try to fight it at first, while things are still good in the marriage, **but if you are diminishing yourself to please your partner**, then you are creating more problems for both of you down the line. If we succumb to the pressure to lose ourselves in the role of wife and mother, it can completely drown the spark you and your husband had.

Finding ways to gain confidence in yourself can be easy. Re-discover hobbies and other pleasures that help you feel more in touch with yourself. Re-affirm every day that your needs are important and get practice expressing your opinions, even when, or maybe especially when, they differ from your husband's so that he will know you are still an individual who is capable of thinking for yourself. But you also need to know this too. You need to be confident and reinforce the things you need with your husband. You need him to know that when you express something, you are doing it with conviction and you're not just some flaky housewife from the 50s who lives to serve. **You are the spicy, interesting woman he married and you are still capable of surprises.**

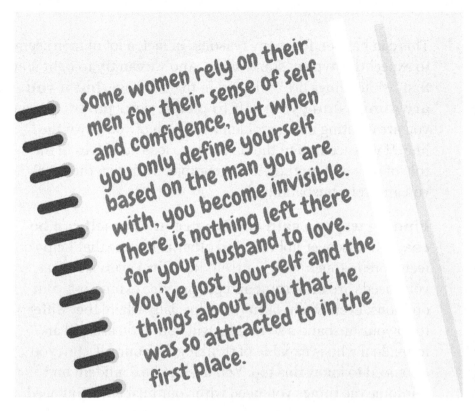

Some women rely on their men for their sense of self and confidence, but when you only define yourself based on the man you are with, you become invisible. There is nothing left there for your husband to love. You've lost yourself and the things about you that he was so attracted to in the first place.

There is a more practical application to increasing your confidence in yourself as well. Through self-expression, we are able to discover that **when we speak, our husband really will listen**. He has made a commitment to you and has honored it for this long – what makes you think he will dismiss your needs when you are able to express them? If he has before, you can open up a line of conversation about it and how it makes you feel. Don't get stuck in a stagnant stereotype of marriage. Stay committed to one another and your feelings. Explain how and why you might resent him for not understanding your needs and forgive him, **also explaining how you have not had the confidence to express them because you are worried it will upset him.**

It's unlikely that your husband doesn't care about you. if you are angry at your husband because he doesn't honor your needs, **really ask yourself if he knows what they are.** Have you been confident enough to express and enforce them? If not, then the problem might be as much yours as it is his, and resenting him for that will be silly. Be straightforward and confident. It can be a very surprising way to improve your marriage and become a better wife. **Most people think of a good wife almost like a slave who will drop everything to serve others.** But a really good wife will understand how to serve herself so that she can put her all into the things that matter – creating loving, lasting memories with her husband.

Chapter 3 – The Importance of **Communication** to Build an Indestructible Family Unit

Who doesn't want a marriage that is as tough as steel? One that will maintain its joy and love for the rest of time, as you and your partner are able to move through the years as if no time has passed at all? Unfortunately, many people have a hard time doing this, but there is a good reason for that. **They don't know how to communicate!**

When we spend a long time with someone, it is often the case that we become afraid of starting conflicts with them. We may be upset about something and refuse to express it because it seems better and easier to overlook these things and maintain the peace.

Focus on the ways you agree more often than the ways you disagree, and when you do disagree, agree to disagree and move on.

You are both separate individuals with your own tastes and preferences, but this is part of what makes your relationship unique.

Most of us are not well trained in conflict resolution, so when we are expressing the things that are serious to us, tensions can become high and we can become emotional or angry and say things we don't mean. We are automatically defensive when people are telling us about our flaws or the ways that we hurt them or are hurt by them, and this can make problem solving very difficult. It can even make it look as if the person who loves you most in the world simply doesn't care about you or the way you feel.

Everybody should be able to feel heard and understood in their relationships. You don't want to build up a life with somebody who will cut you down just to feel superior to you and have only their needs met at all times. This kind of toxic relationship can destroy a person from the inside out.

This is a very frustrating situation to find yourself in. Everybody should be able to feel heard and understood in their relationships. You don't want to build up a life with somebody who will cut you down just to feel superior to you and have only their needs met at all times. This kind of toxic relationship can destroy a person from the inside out.

Fortunately, there are ways that we can begin to take our power back into our own hands and turn these things around. **First of all,** determine whether or not your partner truly is simply selfish and only wants to keep themselves afloat, and if they are not, do your best to become an excellent communicator.

Chances are much higher that your husband wants just as

badly as you do to have a harmonious marriage. If he isn't truly expecting you to diminish yourself to serve him as it might seem many husbands do, then you are going to **truly benefit from opening the lines of communication.**

Something a lot of couples do, especially after a long time of marriage, is to focus a lot on the ways that they <u>disagree or see things differently</u>. You often hear older couples complaining about the ways that they are different or they see the other's opinions or habits as inferior. **This is a damaging and toxic view to have. Your partner is supposed to be the one person who loves you the most through thick and thin,** and focusing on these little differences is one sure-fire way to get you both to bickering or feeling resentful.

Sure, it can be done in good humor, but it shouldn't be the only thing you talk about. It can hurt people's feelings when they are chided in front of their friends and family, or their personal habits become a focal point of someone else's judgment. It can create resentment and become considered micro-aggressions that make it nearly impossible to feel safe to be yourself in your home. This causes a lot of anger toward your partner when what you should really be focusing on **is how much you care about each other.**

There are easy fixes to this. One of these, when you are changing your habits, is to comment on the thing that is different, but follow it up with something that is stronger and more positive. For example, you could say that your husband isn't much for gardening, but he sure does do something else very well. This will probably get him to feeling good about the **observation rather than attacked,** and it will cause a lot less stress on your relationship when this is the case.

19

Another way you can change this is to avoid nitpicking and negative talk in order to focus on the ways that you are similar. It's more important than you would think to find common ground with your partner. While it is great to have your own interests, you also need to find the things that brought you together in the first place – things that you have in common and that you can share. These interests could be anything. A viewpoint, a fun sport or hobby, but the important thing is that it is sincere. Don't try to force yourself to like something your husband likes. Simply focus on the ways that the two of you can get along and be engaged with the other.

You don't want the stale kind of marriage that many people fall victim to. This is a very sad state to find your marriage in, especially when there are easy ways to avoid it. You have to communicate and learn how you and your partner can share more fulfilling activities together. It's one of the most important things in any friendship. While you may have friends who are very different from you, there is something in common that you share that has brought you together. **Make sure you and your husband also have special things to share that can never be taken away from you. Focus on the ways you agree more often than the ways you disagree,** and when you do disagree, agree to disagree and move on. You are both separate individuals with your own tastes and preferences, but this is part of what makes your relationship unique. You can keep each other guessing without making the differences feel like something that will keep you separate and cut off from one another.

Communication is also important because you may not realize it but you and your partner both have needs that each of you can work toward meeting. However, this will never happen without an active interest in your partner. **Ask him**

what he needs and wants! This way, you will be able to truly create a strong and lasting bond that will withstand the test of time!

Chapter 4 – How <u>Compromising</u> Can Change Your Marriage For The Better

Something that can easily go wrong in any relationship is the fact that most of us have ***<u>trouble compromising.</u>*** We grow up knowing that we are the only people who can really tell others what we want and need, ***and sometimes get confused about whether or not the things that we desire are there because we want them or they are there because we actually need to have them.***

<u>The first step</u> in compromise is to begin to understand yourself and whether or not you are able to express needs before desires, and put desires on the back burner when they conflict with the harmony of your marriage. For example, if you feel that you need to perform relationship maintenance or have other ways you would need your spouse to act before you were able to feel loved and appreciated as you deserve to be, those are emotional and possibly physical needs that you have that should be addressed by your partner.

Much of the time we just want to win an argument without thinking about the best possible solution for both of you.

This is when it is time to take a time out and breathe, thinking about how your partner must be feeling about the situation and what would be a good solution for both of you.

However, **if you think you feel the most loved by having expensive gifts lavished upon you and never having to lift a finger, that falls more under the desire category.** Desires can be important, but they should not be the be all end all of your relationship. If they are, they will disrupt the happiness of your marriage and you will both become unhappy.

Learning how to compromise is an essential part of becoming a better partner. Just make sure you're not the only one who is doing the compromising.

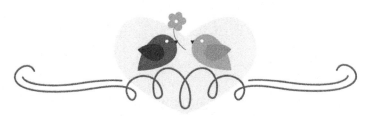

A lot of women compromise themselves immediately, which can also be a problem.

If you are compromising yourself too much, then that means that you are not allowing yourself to have enough say over how you are treated in your relationship.

Compromising is supposed to be able to help you meet your partner halfway so you can both live with the solution to a problem, even if you don't both get exactly what you want. **A lot of the time during arguments, compromise seems nearly impossible because when we are angry our brains shut off and we become stuck on whatever it is that makes us angry.** Much of the time we just want to win an argument without thinking about the best possible solution for both of you. This is when it is time to take a time out and breathe, thinking about how your partner must be feeling about the situation and what would be a good solution for both of you. After all, you have to lay down next to that person at night and wake up with him, spending most of your life at his side.

You might as well try to make it agreeable.

A lot of women compromise themselves immediately, which can also be a problem. They are willing to throw themselves under the bus in order to make their man happy and keep themselves unhappy. But this is another problem and creates perpetual disaster. **If you are compromising yourself too much,** then that means that you are not allowing yourself to have enough say over how you are treated in your relationship. This will create a rift between you and your husband and you may begin to resent him, feeling as though he doesn't care about you and that nothing is going to get better. Because if you don't stop compromising yourself, it won't. you are going to feel terrible all the time.

The previous chapters spoke about how you can begin expressing yourself and building confidence to create a harmonious relationship with your husband. Make sure you allow that advice to really sink in. If your husband truly cares about you, he will want you just as happy as he is in the marriage. And if there are ways you believe he could meet your needs better and ways you feel you could meet his needs better, you can have a conversation about this and learn how you can both compromise to meet these needs without losing things that you value.

When you're not on the same page about something, using advice from the chapter on communication is a great place to begin. Allow yourself to become open-minded to the things he has to say and do what you can to help him meet his needs and yours as well. When you and your partner can compromise, **your relationship will start to feel a whole lot less like work and a whole lot more like a rewarding partnership.**

Both of you will benefit from the difference. Learn to be objective and validate your partner's feelings, even if you don't understand or reciprocate them. Tell him you understand why he may feel the way he does after taking some time to think about it and apologize if you believe you have been inflexible about something. He will probably be very surprised that you were willing to see his side of the subject. It will probably even encourage him to do the same after **he realizes that this is a new, positive habit that can change your marriage around for the better.**

Marriage is a partnership that requires teamwork in order to thrive. You both have to work together to find the best outcome for both parties.

Setting a good example by being the first one to compromise and use phrases such as *"I feel_____ when_____, so I think a good solution would be if we_____. This would help me,"* can be an exceptionally rewarding and influential way of beginning a new, mature phase in your relationship. Take a break from the fighting and the drama.

Get yourself to a quiet place where you can think about the issue without getting angry. And then, once you've calmed down, **think about the things your partner was saying**

and why he might feel the way he feels.

When you return to finish the conversation, surprise him by validating his emotions and letting him know that you are trying to be a better wife and want to find a compromise that will suit you both. It may just become a new era in your marriage that leads to lasting change and growth for the both of you!

Chapter 5 – Enjoying Sex Together

A complaint many women have about their marriages is that sex feels like an obligation. Another complaint many men have about their marriages is that their wives begin to treat sex like an obligation. **Well at one point it was brand new and exciting and fun. So what happened to make the drastic change?**

One thing is for certain. Women's sex drives do not go downhill as they age like men's do. In fact, women continue to evolve sexually and some even speculate that a woman's peak sexual age is much later in life than 20 to 30 years old. As women age, they begin to learn more about what they like and what they want, and if their men are not delivering, sure, sex isn't as exciting anymore. But it could be.

This is where the chapters on honesty and compromise come in handy. The bedroom is the focal point of many marriages. Or at least it was when the coupling began. So if you are not able to truly enjoy yourselves with one another, then there is a high likelihood that you are not being completely honest with each other about what you want and like.

Many women are terrified of expressing their own sexual needs and desires because men are generally considered to be the most dominant in this arena. And while it may bruise your hubby's ego briefly to hear that there are things he could do better, further on down the line, once it sinks in that he can change these things and truly pleasure you, there is a higher likelihood that it will turn him on to know that you are enjoying yourself and that he is the one in control of the pleasure.

If there are things that you have been refusing to even attempt with your husband, things he has always wanted to do, it might also help to explore these options with him in a way that makes you the most comfortable. Maybe you can compromise and do a little bit of something new that each of you want to try out. There are so many opportunities to harness sexual pleasure out there that just a quick internet search might introduce you to things you have never even thought of before. Speak to your husband honestly and candidly about sexual things you'd like to try, or tell him you'd like to have a conversation about sex. **It will be guaranteed to peak his interest. He might even want to start right away!**

As long as you're honest and you start to own your sexuality, you and your partner will quickly begin to enjoy a more fulfilling sex life than ever before. He might be shocked to find out all the things you've been hiding from yourself and from him, and you might be shocked to find out that some of the things he is interested in actually do the trick for you too!

Everybody is different. Especially in the bedroom. The secret is

compromise. Learning how to let go of prudish preconceptions about what sex and purity are supposed to be and just allowing yourself to forgive yourself for not being the perfect little woman that society expects you to be. All you really have to do is find out how to share these things with him in a way that turns him on and before you know it you will both be in a frenzy!

One thing that should always be remembered, even in marriage, is that a woman has the **right to say no** to anything sexual that she doesn't like, even if it has already been initiated. So if you end up not enjoying something your husband wants you to try, you need to ask him to **STOP**. **He should respect you and your needs and be willing to be there for you no matter what. Even if it clashes with what he wants at the time.**

But if you have a great husband who listens and respects you, as all women deserve to be loved and respected, then you will be able to reach a new era of sexual satisfaction in the bedroom. Your husband will be shocked and in awe of realizing that he has such an open-minded and exciting wife, who can overcome what society tells her about being a "good girl" so that she can enjoy herself and his body.

Chapter 6 – <u>Dividing Labor</u> into a System to Avoid Marriage Angst

Something that can really drive people crazy when they are together is an unfair division of labor. If things are not properly taken care of and one person feels that they do more than the other, then there is bound to be resentment. That kind of resentment can be almost impossible to overcome in a marriage, and if there isn't a system in place that works for both of you so that you are able to understand and fulfill your duties and obligations, then there is bound to be conflict somewhere along the way.

Many marriages are divided simply. A man is expected to go to work and bring home all the money, and in exchange his wife is expected to take care of the household chores and children, if there are any. However, times have changed a lot since the 50s and this type of system is clearly unfair. **A woman's work is never done, they say, and that's a fact.**

It is nice to believe that love is strong enough to pull through anything, but unfortunately it is very easy to build up resentment toward somebody that you spend every single day with, even if it is the person that you love most in the world.

Household chores should be divided and a person should be able to be expected to take care of themselves. It's not a woman's job to take care of anybody else, and if your husband or spouse believes that it is your job to care for them, cook and clean and all these other things, even if you have a job of your own, then there are real problems ahead of you.

The best solution here is to consult the communication chapter of this book so that you are confident enough to express how you feel about it when your husband has **<u>unrealistic expectations</u>** of your household responsibilities. You should encourage him to take care of his own needs at times, and divide obligations in a way that both of you can live with. If he works for 8 hours and comes home hungry, of course you can have a meal ready for him. But if you have also been working for 8 hours in the household to make money or to take care of your children or chores, then maybe he could do the dishes afterward. **Find a system that suits you both and stick with it!**

Practical matters can begin to wear a person down after a while. It is nice to believe that love is strong enough to pull through anything, **but unfortunately** it is very easy to build up resentment toward somebody that you spend every single day with, even if it is the person that you love most in the world.

Love isn't enough to keep resentment from building up, whether resentment from your husband or resentment toward him.

Maybe you and your husband can sit down together and make a list of all the things that they are expected to do in the household. When that list is complete, turn it face down and write another list of the things you are expected to do at work or how many hours you work to make money or do other manual labor on your feet, such as cooking and cleaning and chasing children around. Write down how much leisure time you expect you get to yourself during the day to relax in peace. Then compare these totals and discuss the shifts you can make to make life easier on each other so that things are more fair for the both of you.

This is just one example of the way you and your husband can begin to initiate conversations about how to make the

<u>division of labor more fair.</u> That way you can both really see the way you are affecting each other. You can begin to examine systems that could work better for both of you and no matter **what you agree on, you have to stick with it once it is in place.**

If one person gets resentful, you can quickly point out that you both agreed on the system and that it was the most fair way both of you could see to divide labor. If something changes, such as a job status, you can always come back to your system, which you can keep written down and put away in case you need to reference it, so that you can both look it over again and decide what is the most fair thing to do to adjust the system based on the changes that have been made to your schedules.

Overall, it's always important to have a system in place so that you do not begin to feel as though you are carrying more than what is fair of your weight. If your partner begins slacking or you or your partner catches you slacking off, address it and vow to do better.

Move forward instead of backward. Make gentle reminders to each other how difficult it is when you feel the lack of fairness in your routines and encourage each other to keep up the good work. Reward yourselves at the end of the week with some free time together. Maybe you could go out on a date. Whatever you decide, remember to stay devoted to this just as you would be devoted to a work schedule. **It is the work you have to put in to make your marriage work and be a better life.**

Chapter 7 – Earning, Repairing, and Maintaining <u>Trust</u>

When you know somebody long enough, there is a high likelihood that you are going to lose trust in them for one reason or another. Whether they make a lot of well-intentioned promises that are hard for them to follow through on or they have lied or cheated right to our faces, there can be issues within a marriage that make it difficult for us to trust our partners and offer ourselves fully to the person we love the most.

This is a sad situation to find yourself in, but it is still something that you can overcome with persistence and dedication.

A lot of people are able to forgive and forget, but if you are unable to fully trust your partner, there is bound to be a difficult time ahead of you in the future. This can either be avoided or it can cause inevitable problems.

One thing that you can do with your partner is an eye contact exercise that will help you to feel closer to your partner. In order to do this simple exercise to help build trust, you can attempt to stare your partner in their eyes for at least sixty seconds in order to reinforce the importance of maintaining a connection with the windows to your partner's soul.

The best way that you can begin to work through these kinds of issues is to determine whether or not you want to trust your partner again and whether or not your partner can and does want to trust you too. Sometimes people make big mistakes that it seems like it is impossible to recover from, **but if you are dedicated to your partner** and able to work together, it is possible that you and your partner will be able to walk through hell and back, and become all the closer for it.

One thing that you can do with your partner is an eye contact exercise that will help you to feel closer to your partner. In order to do this simple exercise to help build trust, you can attempt to stare your partner in their eyes for at least sixty seconds in order to reinforce the importance of maintaining a connection with the windows to your partner's soul.

It will help you to feel more connected to him, especially if you begin to introduce physical touch. You can hold hands, touch each other's arms, or whatever else you are both comfortable with as you maintain eye contact.

Something else that can build trust after a difficult situation is allowing yourself to open your mind to the idea of couple's counseling. In this environment, if you trust your therapist, you can both begin to sort through your emotional baggage with one another so that you can become a stronger unit as a whole. Sometimes this process can be messy and difficult, but it will usually leave you both with a more clear idea of what you want from each other and out of life in general. It can also help you to organize things such as household tasks and begin to really move through issues that have held you both back from meeting your needs.

Of course, the best way to build trust is to try not to break the trust your partner has in you. It can be very difficult to get that back, and if you never do, your marriage may never be truly fulfilling. Whether you can improve as a wife or not won't matter if you don't trust each other. So be honest about how you feel and work on communicating your needs. Otherwise it may be extremely difficult for you to rekindle what was once shared between you and your husband. When this is the case, sometimes an objective third party can help, such as a therapist.

Either way, try to keep in mind that building trust in someone that has broken it will never happen overnight. You have to want to trust and forgive the person who hurt you, and if you cannot do that, you will have to try harder than ever to repair what was broken or lost. **If that can't be done, it might be better for both of you if you can let**

go of the past and move forward with a <u>fresh start</u>.

But if you are truly hoping to make things work, there are some key points that you should always hold onto in order to make your marriage great again. **The first thing** that should be done is admitting the problem exists. This can often be the hardest part because we want to trust our partners so badly that we can fool ourselves into thinking that we do. It is only when we become really fed up that we begin to see that we have been lying to ourselves about how we feel. This is an indirect lie to our partners as well.

When trust has been broken, it is good to hash it out with your partner. One of the big things that can break up marriages is when a partner cheats. This can be a very painful situation for everyone involved. Many studies show that people who cheat have done so because of a significant **lack of emotional connection** in their marriages, and usually they do not want to be with anybody but their partners. However, it doesn't feel true when it happens, so talking honestly and keeping an open mind about the problem can be a good first step.

If you are the wronged party, try to remember not to ask for too much detail about the thing that has hurt you. **This can prolong the problem and intensify the pain that you experience in relation to it.** When you want to heal from an issue that has been caused by your partner, the last thing you need is to fixate on all of the horrific details of the ways you have been wronged. What needs to happen is utter honesty and staying open to the concept of truly healing.

When you decide that this is what you want, then you should try to keep an open mind to why your partner wronged you. If you are the person who has done the wronging, you need to be willing to drop your defenses and just be honest about how you were feeling rather than acting justified or casual about why you have done something that harmed the person that you love. If you are just getting angry you will prolong the problem and make it impossible to solve, because the person who is hurt will now become extra resentful that you don't seem to care that you have hurt them.

To build trust back up again, you have to be willing to make some sacrifices to your personal freedom for a little while as your partner gets used to having you around again. You have to be willing to make the changes that need to be made and show a noble effort and concrete proof that you are improving. You should be willing to be there to let them know that you are there for them at all times and maintain the integrity of your relationship. There is even a point where, once you are both beginning to feel the effects of the healing process – the wronged party is feeling secure again and the person who has wronged the other is starting to heal from whatever it is that caused them to cause harm – you can renew your vows and spark up the romance as a way of solidifying the lasting changes that you have both made in order to improve your marriage for the better.

And if it is your partner who has wronged you, you do not need to be a better wife and forgive him no matter what; he needs to be a better husband and learn how to build your trust back up again or he will just have to deal with losing you.

However, it is always possible to learn new ways of trusting each other, especially if the problems that you have experienced seem minor in comparison to other breaches of trust. There are so many things that you can do together as a couple that will begin to repair things that feel difficult that you will probably have fun simply exploring all of the options that you have. Make sure your husband is on board and begin to do your best to move forward with the process of healing in order to truly make your marriage work successfully.

Chapter 8 – Considering Your <u>Core Values</u> for a Successful Relationship

Chances are high that you wouldn't have agreed to marry your partner if you knew you didn't share at least a few very major core values. However, sometimes time can take us by surprise and we begin to learn more about the person we've married than we expected to. **Even more surprising can be when we realize that we truly don't agree on some of the most major things that matter to us in life.**

Sure, you can still truly love each other despite these major differences, but it can become a difficult burden to bear when you discover one day, for example, that he truly doesn't want children and you do. Or maybe his religious beliefs truly contradict your own. Or maybe he doesn't feel the same way about food and diet and exercise as you do and is content to do things differently, even though it contradicts the lifestyle you would prefer.

if you are compromising your core
values just to keep the peace, the
unfortunate reality is that you are
going to be much more miserable
and may not even be able to pinpoint
the cause.

These things can be difficult to reconcile, and if you aren't careful they can drive a wedge between you and your partner. And the thing about core values is that they never, if rarely, change. The core values your partner has may always conflict with your own, and vice versa. It can make it very difficult to have a harmonious and successful marriage when you are with someone who just doesn't agree with you in the ways that you both believe are important.

Instead of focusing on the differences that you have, acknowledge the differences. And, more importantly, discover the ways your core values align with those of your partner so that you can move forward together with a stronger bond. If you have core values that align, chances are that much higher that you will both be able to become more comfortable in the relationship knowing that you are moving forward instead of staying stuck behind.

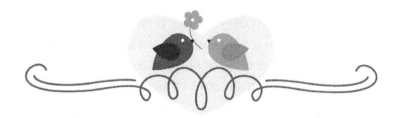

It is common for core values not to align in relationships, but generally the most successful and rewarding relationships are achieved when you are able to enforce your boundaries and be honest with a partner when something doesn't feel right to you.

While you cannot always agree on core values, the fact is that in order to maintain your identity and individuality and remain the same person who your husband fell in love with, you have to hold onto your core values and do your best not to get swept up in his. It might seem important to pretend that you agree, but if you don't, you may quickly find that you are starting to live a lie just to avoid a little bit of conflict with your husband.

This is a dangerous and slippery slope to be on. It can be easy to lose yourself in relationships, especially long lasting ones,

but if you are compromising your core values just to keep the peace, the unfortunate reality is that you are going to be much more miserable and may not even be able to pinpoint the cause.

Your husband loves you for a reason. Because you are yourself. He loves who you are and although it is good to compromise in a relationship, core values can rarely be compromised. Common core values can be explored and expressed in a much more rewarding manner than opposing core values, but in order to maintain an interesting marriage and keep your identity, **you cannot let yourself become worn away by someone else who feels strongly about something you disagree with.**

Your core values are what give you a definition of what is meaningful in your life. We all have certain rules and boundaries, and perspectives that make us the unique individuals that we are. If you are not willing or able to deal with oppositions in your core values, that is because they are sometimes invasive of your boundaries and the things you find acceptable in another person.

It is common for core values not to align in relationships, but generally the most successful and rewarding relationships are achieved when you are able to enforce your boundaries and be honest with a partner when something doesn't feel right to you.

Honoring our core values is important. If we are unable to do honor the things about us that we truly care about, then we are not being fair to ourselves. Even if we think we can compromise and try to find happiness in our relationship without honoring our core values, in the long run it hurts us even if we don't realize it. **In fact, <u>losing sight of who</u>**

you truly are is one of the most common ways that marriages begin to fall apart. Stay true to yourself in order to be a better wife! It may seem like harmony and compromise is always the answer, but not when it comes to core values.

You can't usually change yours and you probably can't change your partner's either. The best thing to do in a situation where they don't line up is to **find the ways that you do agree and focus on those instead of letting the differences tear you apart or losing sight of what you value altogether.**

It's okay if you disagree. What is difficult is finding yourself again once you begin to lose sight of the things that truly matter to you. When that happens, your husband will most likely lose respect for you because you are unable to think for yourself. But what is worse than that is when you begin to lose respect for yourself because you just know that you are not honoring the parts of yourself that demand respect and understanding and compliance. **When we don't respect ourselves, we begin to feel miserable and worthless.** That sometimes leads into toxic relationships because you are not willing to stand up for yourself and you invite people to treat you disrespectfully.

It's all right to disagree with your partner and their core values, and if you fight because you disagree sometimes that is okay. Your husband needs to know where you truly stand. However, if the fights are serious, frequent, and draining, you can still hold onto your core value, **but you will need to change the way you communicate it.** If you have a mature partner who doesn't need you to think exactly the same way as he does, then you should feel comfortable expressing yourself. As long as you are able to agree to disagree with your partner, things will be all right in the end. Sometimes that takes maturity that isn't quite there yet, **but by focusing on the ways you are similar rather than the ways you are different,** you can maintain your values and get along when your partner's core values are different than yours.

It is more likely that people are hurt when their values appear to be trampled on, so show respect to your partner and their values even if you do not agree with them completely for yourself.

Marriage is a compromise, but instead of compromising your core values, compromise by allowing yourself to support your partner no matter what their values are if they are willing to do the same.

Chapter 9 – Mature <u>Conflict Resolution</u> for Better Relationships

Every couple fights now and again. When we disagree, usually it's easy to move on with our lives. Other times, we are both angry and really need to feel heard by the other person. When that doesn't happen, conflict can be engaged in for hours or create a serious rift between people who otherwise just want to make each other happy and enjoy their lives together. When we fight like this without proper resolution, our needs are less likely to be met and we will be a lot more dissatisfied in our marriages and relationships in general.

Learning better conflict resolution skills can help you in every aspect of your life. We all have different experiences that lead us to act or react a certain way to specific situations, and **if we are not very good at managing these conflicts they can quickly escalate beyond repair.** The saddest thing about this is that we usually want to have the conflicts ending so that we can move on with our lives, but forgiving and forgetting and letting go to the anger we feel when we are wronged can be one of the hardest things to do, especially when we are angry.

While upset, the blood that is usually circulating in our brains and allowing us to think clearly is stopped short, leaving us unreasonable and angry more often than not. We begin to think in extremities and if we let our anger speak for us, as so many people unfortunately do, the tensions grow higher and the stakes begin to feel insurmountable.

Many people say things they don't mean while they feel this way and it can be extremely difficult for them to repair the damage that has been done while they are angry, and even more difficult to encourage your partner to trust you again once things that are <u>best left unsaid are brought into light.</u> **Just because our angry brains think it's a good thing to say, doesn't mean it is, and usually we want to repair conflict right away.**

Some people are actually addicted to conflict, and these people will probably never be open to mature problem solving and conflict resolution, because they feel the most important while they are angry. The rage gives them a sense of power and control, and if they are outraged and playing the victim, this type of toxic mindset is not going to help to build a healthy foundation for a relationship. Take a moment to think honestly to yourself about this, whether you ever admit it to anyone else or not. Are you addicted to high-stakes conflict?

If you are, don't worry. You are not alone. There is also help for you out there if you are willing to reach out for it. Hopefully some of the advice in this book will help, but if you do have a legitimate mental addiction to stress and conflict, there may be more benefits to seeking professional therapy in order to help you to maintain healthier relationships.

This is a frequent struggle many people have to deal with, especially if they grew up in tumultuous environments. Our past has a way of affecting our present relationships, so make sure that you are willing and able to move forward with as much gusto as you can possibly get! The easiest way to ensure this is to be honest with yourself.

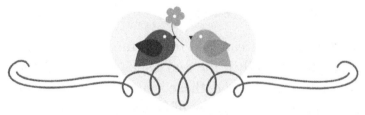

Learning better conflict resolution skills can help you in every aspect of your life. We all have different experiences that lead us to act or react a certain way to specific situations, and if we are not very good at managing these conflicts they can quickly escalate beyond repair.

If there are other things that may be causing the conflicts in your relationship, then don't worry! There are ways that you can begin to improve your conflict resolution abilities. **Most people are terrified of fighting because they see it as the beginning of the end.** Unfortunately, there is sometimes so much stigma about fighting that the real issues never get fully expressed and both parties live with exasperation and grudges that have built up for so long that it's nearly impossible for them to move forward.

The resentment has built up for so long that there are never going to be constructive solutions that will work to repair the relationship, and this is one of the saddest situations that you can find yourself in. Especially if you genuinely care for the person that you're with.

Petty resentments can lead to constant bickering in a marriage, especially if the real issues are never tended to. Over the course of time, these issues will continue to pile up and cause both of you a lot of harm. This is never a good thing and you are generally going to have to decide what is more important – the façade of peace or truly uncovering the dark underbelly of your relationship so that you can begin to move onto a path of healing with your partner.

Most people think they would choose a path of healing, but it is much harder than it looks. Sometimes, learning conflict resolution to avoid more problems is all you need. **You can leave the past aggressions behind as you begin to grow more comfortable being honest with your partner about the things that are bothering you and why.** Everybody needs help solving their problems maturely at times, but when you are able to do so there is nothing more rewarding in the world than being able to look into the eyes of the person you love and thanking them for being honest with you about what the trouble was and mature enough to find a solution that makes you both feel happy and loved.

When we care for someone we do not want to hurt them with the difficulties of our lives and our anger. This is why so many people avoid talking about these issues all together. We don't want to create conflict with the people who are most important to us. But unfortunately, **conflict exists for a reason and without it we are unable to live our lives with complete honesty.** Women in general are told from an early age not to make waves, so this can be even harder for wives. Women who have been expected to submit for so long are not used to expressing difficult or extreme emotions during conflict, so it can come out very messy and immaturely at times, <u>maybe lending to why so many people consider women hysterical or over-emotional.</u> Anybody would be if they were not allowed to express their true values and needs for such a long time.

At any rate, these problems can be quickly resolved if only you and your partner are willing to be patient with one another as you learn a new way of problem solving. This type of conflict resolution is generally going to leave you both with better solutions to your problems so that neither one of you will feel obligated to compromise too much of your values. Better yet, you will both feel heard and validated and avoid all of the nonsense that comes along with the reality of our brains not receiving the proper amount of blood to begin problem solving strategies.

The first place to start is to take a few deep breaths and calm down. When you sense a conflict on the rise and about to escalate, do whatever you can to calm yourself and maintain your center to avoid conflict. Many people who are acting impulsively and with anger are quick to attack the other person rather than trying to solve problems. If you are insulting or degrading your partner or vice versa, it is only going to rightfully escalate the problem. Neither of you deserve to be treated with disrespect over a conflict that could be dealt with maturely.

It is the issue at hand that needs to be dealt with. It is not fair to attack somebody personally when it has nothing to do with the issue. Even if you think their incompetence has everything to do with the issue, nothing will be solved by putting others down and resorting to bullying. It is a very immature and toxic way to go about solving problems, and it is a <u>**learned behavior that needs to be unlearned**</u> so that you (or your partner) will be able to solve problems maturely like an adult rather than a damaged child.

It is okay for you to feel angry, but it is not okay to attack the person you are angry at personally. Many couples learn a lot by reading to their partners what they say in a disagreement, switching the roles around so that they each understand how the other is affected by their words.

Difficulties in relationships are normal. We all think and feel extreme things about others that we spend too much time with, especially if we are not in the habit of solving problems maturely. **Attacks on your personal character, habits, past, and beliefs can all feel extremely personal, and if not worded carefully are even cruel at times.** But if you are able to learn from your challenges and allow the problems that you have as a couple to season you and help you grow to truly appreciate one another and change for the best, then you are going to have a much easier time throughout the rest of your live when it comes to solving your problems.

Most people hope to grow as couples without having to resolve their differences. They don't realize when they first enter into a relationship just how difficult it can truly be to learn to live with another person, especially if you were not given a proper example of how to show love or deal with conflict by your parents. Everybody has a hard time in ways with this concept, especially if they are not fully able to process their feelings quickly. It can be extremely difficult to understand our thoughts and feelings, which makes conflict even more messy when we can't sort it out for ourselves right away.

A lot of people have a hard time
exercising that type of self-control,
and it can cause a lot of conflict in
the relationships that they are in.
Staying mindful of the way you
affect your partner can have amazing
rewards and benefits right away.

This is where positive conflict resolution will come in handy. This may turn out to be the longest chapter in the book because it is probably the most important one in maintaining a healthy and harmonious marriage. Both parties should feel heard and be comfortable expressing their thoughts and feelings to the other person. We have to learn how to accept criticism graciously, especially when it means changing the way we behave so that we are more conscientious of our partners and their needs.

It is okay for you to feel angry, but it is not okay to attack the person you are angry at personally. Many couples learn a lot by reading to their partners what they say in a disagreement, switching the roles around so that they each understand how the other is affected by their words.

This can be a powerful exercise, but one that is most likely to be properly effective with a professional third party to help you to understand the emotions that can arise from a difficult situation such as the one you are experiencing. **However, try to think of this before you say anything at all.** If what you want to say would throw you into a rage or hurt you deeply, remember, even if you're not feeling warm and fuzzy toward your partner in the moment, you do not want to do or say things that will hurt them.

Sometimes it can actually be worse to try and solve conflicts right in the throes of angry and difficult emotions, especially when one or both of you are having a hard time in processing your extreme emotions.

A lot of people have a hard time exercising that type of self-control, and it can cause a lot of conflict in the relationships that they are in. Staying mindful of the way you affect your partner can have amazing rewards and benefits right away. However, there are other keys to utilizing successful conflict resolution strategies that can also help you both in building a better future together.

The main thing is to remember that you love each other, and if you are angry there is an issue behind the anger that is upsetting both of you. Communicating clearly about how you feel and asking your husband how he feels and why can be a very successful first step in conflict resolution. It can be surprising to have your feelings validated right away, and it is one of the most successful things that you can do in order to ensure that the problem you are having does not escalate.

When we indulge in our anger, sure, we feel more powerful, but we also feel more justified in hurting others and saying things we may not necessarily mean. These things said in anger generally draw attention away from the real issue, escalate the conflict, and create more barriers to solving the problem at hand. Soon the argument goes far off point and you are fighting about something else entirely.

You really have to learn the laws of communication before this step can be successful though. Using "I" statements in order to avoid placing the blame on other people can be remarkably effective. **You want to draw attention to the real issue and not the anger that you feel.** When we indulge in our anger, sure, we feel more powerful, but we also feel more justified in hurting others and saying things we may not necessarily mean. These things said in anger generally draw attention away from the real issue, escalate the conflict, and create more barriers to solving the problem at hand. **Soon the argument goes far off point and you are fighting about something else entirely.**

Sometimes when two people are just too hot-headed to deal with their relationship arguments and don't want to hurt each other with their words, it is a good idea to take a break. Many professionals used to suggest not going to bed angry at each other. They said to hash things out immediately. But recent studies have begun to show that this is bad advice. **It is actually better to give each other space and time to work through the core issues in your head and sleep off the high tensions from the night before.** If that means one of you spends a night or two on the couch, then that is just how it will have to be to have a successful marriage.

Sometimes it can actually be worse to try and solve conflicts right in the throes of angry and difficult emotions, especially when one or both of you are having a hard time in processing your extreme emotions. Don't be afraid to take a break from the argument. Let your spouse know that you are in need of some space so you can get a clear head and address the situation properly when things are beginning to feel better for you. Don't push your partner if he asks you to take a break from the fight so that he can organize his thoughts. If things are beginning to get heated, in fact, you should recommend that you both disengage and give yourselves a chance to think more calmly and rationally about the issue at hand.

Once you're both a little bit more level headed, you can start the next conversation off on a loving note. Let your partner know you care for him and would do anything it takes to ensure the stability of your relationship, but that there are ways you are hurt by what is going on and things that you need addressed. Let him know you have thought about his side of things and at this point, maybe both of you will be more likely and willing to compromise together to find a solution that works best for both of you to whatever issue it is that you are having. If the issue seems unresolvable, try to inject humor into it and see what you can do to agree to disagree. If one of you has to make a sacrifice, be willing to think objectively over which one of you will lose more, even if that person is you.

There are going to be times where this can feel impossible, but don't worry. After a bit of practice, **conflict resolution becomes a stronger skill.** And as you learn and grow with your partner, individual habits become patterns that you can predict and prepare for in order to avoid conflicts.

Many couples have the hardest adjustment periods when they are first together, and this happens for a variety of reasons. Most people are simply not used to sharing so many aspects of their lives with someone who, in many ways, is still a virtual stranger. You have to be willing to put your love first and work through the issues that arise in your relationship so that the conflicts you experience will not be the aspect of your marriage that holds the most weight. Make as many happy and positive memories as possible to balance out the heavy weight of your difficult emotions.

Through compromise and mature problem solving, you and your partner should be able to move on from conflicts with a clear head and do whatever it takes to **go on living as a team rather than divided by silly issues.** If you do not learn ways to constructively solve problems, then you are bound to make each other miserable, and that misery can affect you both profoundly throughout the long haul.

Simply lead by example and let him know that there needs to be a break to gather your thoughts so you can consider his point of view.

It can be surprising to have a receptive person during an argument, and it can de-escalate the tensions right away. It may even soften your partner immediately so that he explains more calmly and evenly why he is upset and how the situation affects him so that you can consider his opinion and point of view more carefully. Encourage him to do so if he begins and if you can bring your own anger down enough to engage him right away, do so. <u>It may be the end of the fight!</u>

Whatever you do, avoid name-calling and over-generalizing. Stick only to the issue at hand and don't let other built up resentments pile in and cloud your judgment.

If you are mad that your partner has been slacking off with his chores, stick with the chore issue. **Don't bring his lazy, worthless nature into it or the way his parents coddled him and spoiled him and made him**

practically useless. That will add several layers of anger and pain to the conflict that doesn't need to be there.

All you need to address is the way it affects you when the dishes aren't attended to properly, and how you would appreciate it if he would try to keep up, because neither of you like it when you have to nag. This approach will be <u>guaranteed to get better results</u> than bringing a whole lot of personal <u>attacks into the mix and you will get what you want far more quickly with far less hassle.</u>

Focus on the issue and the solution! Nothing else! At least, not if you actually care about solving problems more than you enjoy feeling superior and powerful in your anger.

Conclusion

Over the course of time, we often begin to see ways that we are not fully supporting our partners and ways we feel we are lacking in our relationships. This can be a scary discovery to make, especially if you feel like you are just one wrong step away from losing your marriage and everything you hold dear. However, there are so many ways that you can address relationship difficulties that you will be more likely to resolve them easily using the advice in this book.

When you're arguing, listen to his point of view. If he is struggling with something, put yourself out there to see how you can help him. Do what it takes to show him that you are there for him and that no matter what, you are willing to work through your problems together as a couple and maintain a harmonious marriage.

Stay true to who you are and remember that you only get one life to live. If you are living it to make someone else happy and forgetting yourself, you're doing it wrong. That isn't what marriage is all about.

Learning how to resolve conflicts maturely is a huge step in any relationship, so make sure that you get enough practice at this to be able to truly show growth and change in this arena. If you guys are spending too much time together, go ahead and get yourself a hobby so that every little thing he says doesn't irritate you. If he is irritating you for other reasons, such as unexpressed angers and resentments that have built up over the years that make you intolerant of him, maybe you can participate in couple's counseling or a long heart to heart where you tell each other whatever it is that is bothering you. This can be difficult and messy though, so an objective third party can be beneficial.

Overall, staying true to yourself is the best way you can be a better wife. Never compromise yourself and your core values for anybody. But you should definitely be able to let your partner know where you stand and that you support him even if he disagrees.

Never let anybody tell you how to think or feel. Learn how to communicate your feelings and needs clearly and maturely, with respect, love, and humor. These are the tricks to marriage that so few people talk about. Maybe because there are not a lot of people who understand. **It can be easy to lose yourself in any relationship.** But chances are your husband wants you exactly how you were when you met. He doesn't want the person who bends over like a twig to please him. **Stay true to who you are and remember that you only get one life to live. If you are living it to make someone else happy and forgetting yourself, you're doing it wrong. That isn't what marriage is all about.**

Marriage is the union of two people who care about each other and want to learn how to navigate life together as partners. When you and your husband truly get in tune with one another, there is nothing greater than the feeling you get knowing that the person by your side will stick with you no matter what. **Your love will stand the test of time.**

****

Did you enjoy reading this book? Can I ask you a favour?

Thanks for purchasing and reading this book, I really hope you find it helpful.

If you find this book helpful, **<u>please help others find this book by kindly leaving a review.</u>** I love getting feedback from my customers, loved it or hated it! Just Let me know. and I would really appreciate your thoughts.

Thanks in advance

Jennifer N. Smith

Check out my website below for more self-improvement tips and advice:

http://improve-yourself-today.com/

Did you enjoy reading
this book?

Please help others
find this book by
kindly leaving a
review.

Thanks in advance

Jennifer N. Smith

ABOUT THE AUTHOR

For me, the hardest part of being a mom is learning how to manage my own emotions. After having a baby, I found myself yelling at my husband and my son every day, I felt horrible and guilty afterward, and I felt so stressed and tired all the time.

I started reading lots of self-help books and I have learned a lot. Now, I feel happier and positive.

I want to share what I have learned throughout the years with my readers; I hope my books can help you deal with your day-to-day challenges, and make you feel happy again, you can create a home full of peace and love for the whole family.

Made in the USA
Las Vegas, NV
24 February 2022